Life Lessons for the
GRADUATE
Some Stuff to Know!

TROY JOHNSON

Bristol Park Books

First Bristol Park Edition published in 2018

Bristol Park Books
252 West 38th Street
New York, NY 10018

Bristol Park Books is a registered trademark
of Bristol Park Books, Inc.

Library of Congress Control Number: 2017957024

ISBN: 978-0-88486-678-7

E-Book ISBN: 978-0-88486-679-4

Text and cover design by Keira McGuinness
Cover art copyright ©2018 AllNikArt/Shutterstock

Printed in Malaysia

To

Beautiful Ella

From

Love, Jackie

Sending you all the
very best wishes for
an amazing future!

Go ahead and celebrate! You deserve it. You've reached that first milestone along the journey. And you don't have to have it all figured out.

Just walking into life's journey will help define your next steps. But for now, it's time to celebrate your accomplishments. Take a big sigh of relief and enjoy the moment. You have a lot of life in front of you!

Congratulations!

Opportunity

OPPORTUNITY QUIETLY SURROUNDS YOU. INFORMATION AND KNOWLEDGE ARE WITHIN REACH. PROSPERITY IS SILENTLY KNOCKING AT YOUR DOOR. SUCCESS IS AVAILABLE.

Know who you are and stay true to who you are. These are the things that really matter.

Too many people come to the fountain of life with a glass instead of a pitcher...a teaspoon instead of a steam shovel. They expect little and get little in return.

Whatever you do, do it with all your might.
Work at it, early and late. In season and out
of season, not leaving a stone unturned.

Get more sleep each night. Begin a program of
regular, sensible exercise. Avoid harmful food and
drink. And find a way to make stress a choice.

You are the sole owner of your own talents and opportunities. You have been given your own particular gifts—the rest is up to you.

Priorities

LEARN TO PUT FIRST THINGS FIRST. **START WITH A PASSION TO EXCEL.** FOCUS YOUR PASSION ON WHAT'S MORE IMPORTANT.

With your priorities in place,
you are much more ready
to tackle and achieve
your goals.

Big decisions have big consequences.
Think about the consequences now,
or you may pay a big price later.

Vision without execution is seeing but not believing. Don't let your dreams fall to the side because you didn't pursue them.

You have a unique array of talents and opportunities. If you use your gifts wisely, they multiply. If you misuse them or ignore them, they can be lost.

Simplicity and peace are two concepts that are closely related. Complexity and peace are not.

It's easy to put off unpleasant tasks until "later." Do the unpleasant work first. Then you can enjoy the rest of your day.

Diligence

SEIZE THE GOOD OPPORTUNITY WHEN YOU CAN. TOMORROW MAY BE TOO LATE.

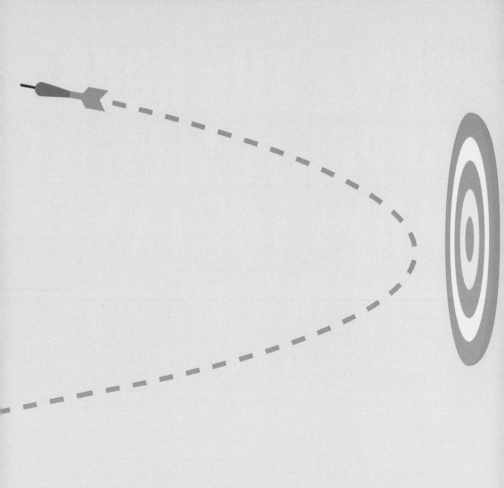

When you take a disciplined approach to your life and your responsibilities, your rewards will be greater than you expected.

No matter how badly you may fail
(and it will happen), just get
back up and begin again.
A second chance
opportunity is
waiting for you
to respond.

*Stop and ask for directions,
then follow the instructions.
Stay on the guided path and
eventually you'll arrive!*

*When you build on your strengths,
the activities using those strengths
come easily to you.
To achieve your dream(s),
you have to build on
those strengths.*

Everyone has problems. How you approach your problems — avoid them or address them — determines how successfully you will overcome them. Life is an exercise in perseverance.
If you persevere, you win!

Don't wait for enthusiasm to find you ... go looking for it. Look at your life and your relationships as exciting adventures.

Encouragement

ENCOURAGEMENT OFFERS HOPE. AND HOPE IS CONTAGIOUS. ASSOCIATE WITH HOPE-FILLED PEOPLE. IF YOU SPEND TIME WITH NAYSAYERS, PESSIMISTS, AND CYNICS, YOUR THOUGHTS CAN BECOME NEGATIVE.

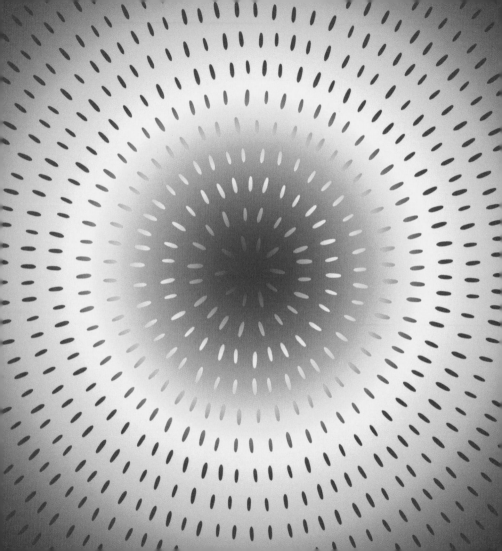

Acquire the habit of hopeful thinking.
Live for today, but hold your hands
open to tomorrow.

There is a seed of hope in every event,
circumstance, and situation in which
you find yourself.

Everyone needs encouragement. Everyone who receives encouragement is changed by it. When things go wrong, it's easy to become discouraged.

Those who discover a path of hope find a great road of encouragement.

When you do the right thing, even if you don't receive a blessing from it, it will feel like you did.

Develop a pattern of thinking that allows you to embrace the promises of today while looking forward to the hope of tomorrow.

Attitude

YOU ARE NOT WHAT YOU THINK YOU ARE. WHAT YOU THINK, YOU ARE.

*If you go into an undertaking expecting
to succeed, the odds are you'll succeed.
if you go in fear of losing, you're more
likely to lose.*

*Attitudes are contagious.
Another person can help
you shoot higher,
laugh louder, and look
forward to tomorrow.*

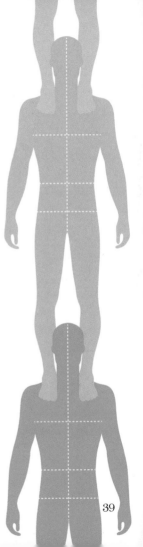

39

You cannot see the future.
Let your instincts, beliefs,
and actions be your guide
along life's journey.

First you make choices.
Soon those choices
will shape your life.

Make smart choices…
or face the consequences
of making dumb ones.

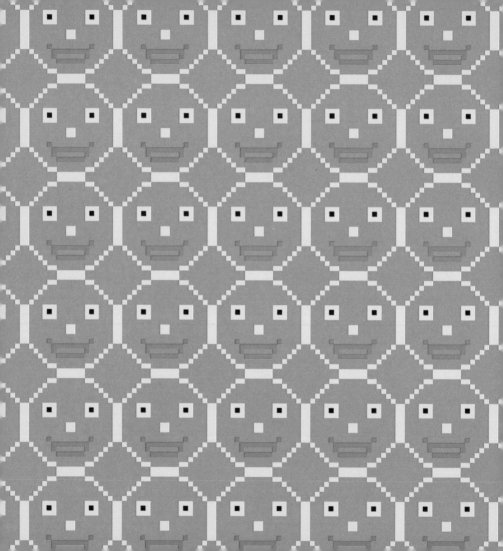

When you make a mistake fix it.

Better now, not later.

The sooner you address it the better.

Don't let it become a larger issue.

Learn to laugh.

Life has a light side—look for it.

Laughter is medicine for the soul,

so take your medicine early and often.

Fill yourself with gratitude.
When you do, there's simply
no room left for complaints.

Pressures can be good or bad.
The more you seek out and
experience the good, the less
you have to deal with the bad.

Core
Integrity

INTEGRITY IS
BUILT SLOWLY
OVER A LIFETIME.
IT IS A CORE VALUE.
SEEK TO LIVE EACH
DAY WITH HONESTY
AND ETHICS.

Don't try to live the life that marketing and advertising companies can misguide you into. You will spend too much time trying to be someone other than who you really are.

The real test of integrity is being willing to tell the truth when it's hard, and own up to it.

Listen carefully to your conscience.
When you do, your actions will be honorable
and your core will take care of itself.
It's the thoughts of the heart that
shape a person's life.

When you realize that this world
is not all about generating financial gain
to satisfy your wants,
your outlook on how you
spend your money
begins to change.

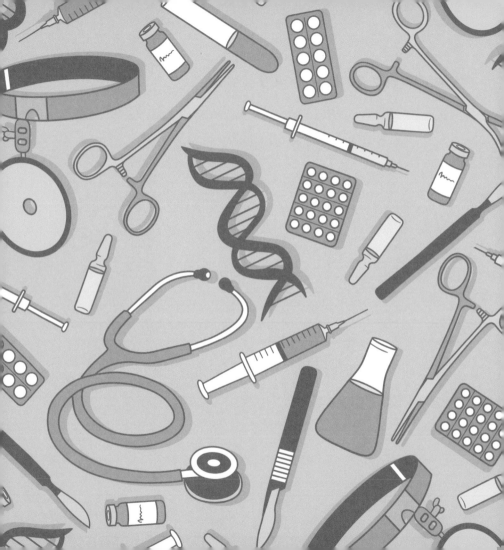

Simply put, it's up to you
to assume the ultimate responsibility
for your health and well-being.

Be ready to serve at a moment's notice.
Are you prepared for an opportunity
to serve and help make a difference?

Because actions do speak louder than words,
it's always a good time to let your actions
speak for themselves.

Beware of telling "white" lies.
Sometimes we're tempted to shade the truth.
Little white lies have a tendency
to turn dark and grow larger.
Avoid untruths of all sizes and colors.

When your conscience says "no,"
that is a good thing.
Listen to your conscience.
Trust it to lead you when
answering "yes" or "no."

Character

CHARACTER IS BUILT SLOWLY OVER A LIFETIME. IT IS FORGED ON THE ANVIL OF HONORABLE WORKS AND POLISHED BY THE TWIN VIRTUES OF GENEROSITY AND HUMILITY.

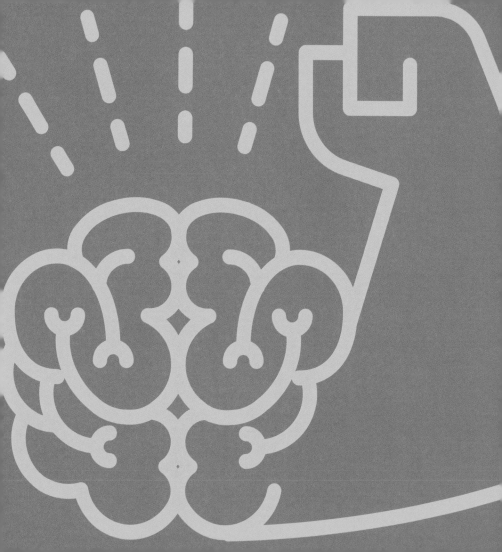

If you strive to gain character,
seek to live each day with
discipline, honesty, and belief.
When wealth is lost, nothing is lost.
When health is lost, something is lost.
When character is lost, all is lost.

Think of something important that you've been putting off. Then think of your excuses to avoid the responsibility. What can you do to finish what you've been avoiding?

Increase your supply of courage by sharing it. As you interact with friends, family, and others, share your courage, your hopes, your dreams, and your enthusiasm.

When it comes to mentors, you need them. When it comes to mentoring, they need you.

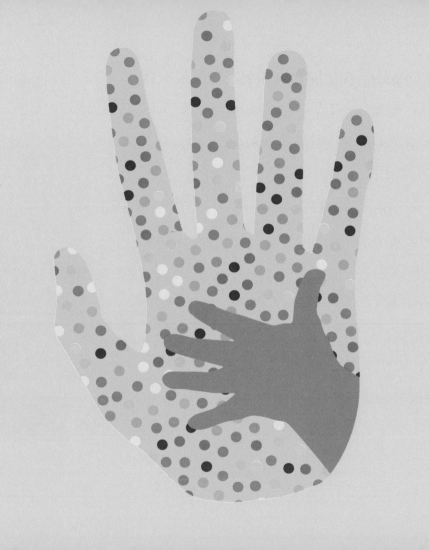

The more you help others,
the better you'll feel about yourself.
Somebody needs your help today.

Use your experiences—both good and bad—to
learn, to grow, to share, and to teach.

Aim High

CHOOSE TO DREAM BIG. STRIVE TO REACH THE FULL POTENTIAL OF YOUR LIFE. CHOOSE TO FOCUS ON THE IMPORTANT ISSUES OF LIFE.

Most people spend their lives
lowering buckets into empty wells
and waste their days pulling them
up, empty, again and again.

If you're about to make a big decision
or take a significant risk,
get advice from people you trust
and value their insight.

The world's power to distract and detour is like rush hour traffic. You have the right to steer clear of on-coming distractions.

The Journey Ahead

Commit to personal growth.

Success doesn't come from acquiring, achieving,
or advancing. It comes as a result of growing.
If you make it your goal to grow, you will see
positive results in your life.

Value the process more than the destination.

The process of change and growth has lasting value.
If you want to go on to the next level, strive for
continual improvement.

Don't wait for days when you feel good.

Motivate yourself to achieve life's best,

regardless of how you feel on a given day.

To be successful, you must persevere.

Be willing to sacrifice your wants.

There are many "opportunity costs" that life presents.

For everything in life, you pay a price. You choose to

pay it on the front end or the back end. If you pay first,

you can enjoy greater rewards in the end.

Dream big.

It doesn't pay to dream small. Be aware that
the potential that exists in you is limitless
and largely untapped.

Plan your priorities.

Successful people have mastered the ability to manage
their time. First and foremost, they have organized
themselves. Every minute spent in planning saves two
in execution. You never regain lost time, so make
the most of every moment.

It's going to be an incredible journey.

Sometimes it will be exciting, other times only

discipline can carry you through. Always remember

that success is waiting for you to make the first move.

Enjoy!

Illustration Credits